Published By Robert Corbin

@ Terry Duke

The Carnivore Diet: the Best Kept Secrets of How to Feel Great, Take Control of Your Weight, and Unleash Your Inner Carnivore

All Right RESERVED

ISBN 978-87-94477-85-7

TABLE OF CONTENTS

turkey And Bacon Rollups 1

Grilled Chicken And Cheese Quesadilla 2

Beef And Broccoli Stir Fry 4

Balsamic Glaze 7

Almond Butter Cookies 9

Grilled Steak: 11

Baked Chicken Breasts 13

Bacon Wrapped Pork Tenderloin 15

Filet Mignon And Mushroom Eggs Skillet 17

Sirloin Steak And Vegetable Eggs Skillet 19

Roasted Vegetables 21

Grilled Shrimp 22

Baked Cod With Lemon And Herbs 23

Stuffed Bell Peppers With Ground Beef And Cheese 25

Bacon Wrapped Pork Chops 28

Beef Jerky: 29

Delicious Beef Tacos 31

Mustard Chuck Roast 32

Sandwich Recipe 33

Korean Steamed Egg With Machaca Recipe 35

Breakfast Tacos Recipe... 37

Tasty Chuck Roast 39

Savory Shredded Beef 40

Meatballs... 42

Pizza... 44

Sausage And Scrambled Eggs 46

Casserole 48

Stuffed Portobello Mushrooms With Ground Beef And Cheese 51

Herbroasted Chicken Thighs 54

Classic Baconwrapped Scallops....................................... 56

Garlicherb Baconwrapped Scallops................................. 58

Mapleglazed Baconwrapped Scallops............................. 61

Banana Cake 64

Salted Caramel Apple Tart... 66

- Chocolate Peanut Butter Pie: 68
- Chimichurri Sauce 70
- Homemade Ranch Dressing 72
- Spicy Mustard Sauce 74
- Bacon Wrapped Shrimp With Spicy Mayo Dipping Sauce 76
- Grilled Salmon With Lemon And Herb Butter 78
- Stuffed Mushrooms 80
- Zucchini Noodles 82
- Keto Chocolate Mousse 84
- Spaghetti Carbonara 86
- Lasagna Bolognese 87
- Pizza 90
- Steak Nuggets With Chipotle Ranch Dip 94
- Cheesy Air Fryer Meatballs Recipe – Keto & Carnivore . 97
- Beef Stew Meat 99
- Steak Bites 101
- Tasty Flank Steak 103

Sausage And Cheese Omelet	107
Salmon And Avocado	109
Greek Style Grilled Lamb Chops	111
Baked Lemon Herb Salmon	114
Classic Garlic Butter Mushrooms	116
Lemon Herb Garlic Butter Mushrooms	118
Balsamic Glazed Garlic Butter Mushrooms	121
Coconut Bacon Bits	124
Coconut Whipped Cream	125
Coconut Flour Brownies	126
Baked Sweet Potato Fries	128
Lemon Garlic Butter Sauce	130
Blackened Salmon Filet	132
Sizzling Fajitas With Chicken, Steak Or Shrimp	133
Bbq Ribs With Homemade Sauce	137
Vanilla Panna Cotta	140
Coconut Fat Bombs	142
Baconchocolate Bark	144

Gnocchi With Meat Ragout 146

Lentil Soup With Sausage 149

Risotto Alla Milanese With Ossobuco 151

Carnivore Fried Chicken Strips 154

Ultra Simple Carnivore Diet Bone Broth Recipe 157

Turkey And Bacon Rollups

Ingredients:

- 1 lb turkey slices
- 4 oz cream cheese, softened
- 8 slices of bacon, cooked until crispy

Directions:

1. Lay out the turkey slices on a clean surface.
2. Spread a thin layer of softened cream cheese on each turkey slice.
3. Place a slice of crispy bacon on top of each turkey slice, positioning it parallel to one edge.
4. Roll up each turkey slice tightly, enclosing the bacon and cream cheese.
5. Secure the rolls with toothpicks if needed.

6. Serve your Turkey and Bacon RollUps as a delicious and portable lunch or appetizer option!

Grilled Chicken And Cheese Quesadilla

Ingredients:

- 4 large flour tortillas
- 2 cups shredded cheddar cheese
- 1/2 cup chopped onion
- 1/2 cup chopped bell pepper
- 1/4 cup chopped fresh cilantro
- 2 boneless, skinless chicken breasts
- 1 tablespoon olive oil
- Salt and pepper
- 1/4 cup sour cream (optional)

Directions:

1. Preheat a grill or grill pan to medium high heat.
2. Brush the chicken breasts with olive oil and season with salt and pepper.
3. Grill the chicken for about 56 minutes per side, or until cooked through. Let rest for a few minutes, then slice thinly.
4. Lay a tortilla flat on a cutting board and sprinkle with about 1/2 cup of shredded cheese. Top with a quarter of the sliced chicken, onion, bell pepper, and cilantro.
5. Sprinkle with an additional 1/4 cup of cheese, then fold the tortilla in half to create a half moon shape.
6. Repeat with the remaining tortillas and Ingredients:.
7. Place the quesadillas on the grill and cook for 23 minutes per side, or until the cheese is melted and the tortilla is crispy.

8. Slice each quesadilla into quarters and serve hot with a dollop of sour cream, if desired.
9. Enjoy your delicious and protein packed Grilled Chicken and Cheese Quesadilla!

Beef And Broccoli Stir Fry

Ingredients:

- 1 tsp fresh ginger, grated

- 1/4 cup soy sauce

- 1 tbsp cornstarch

- 1 tbsp brown sugar

- 1/4 cup water

- 1 lb beef sirloin, thinly sliced

- 1 large head of broccoli, cut into small florets

- 2 tbsp vegetable oil

- 2 cloves garlic, minced

- Salt and pepper, to taste

Directions:
1. Heat the vegetable oil in a wok or large skillet over high heat.
2. Add the sliced beef to the pan and cook for 35 minutes, until browned and cooked through. Remove from the pan and set aside.
3. In the same pan, add the broccoli florets and cook for 23 minutes until tendercrisp. Remove from the pan and set aside with the beef.
4. In the same pan, add the minced garlic and grated ginger and cook for 30 seconds, until fragrant.
5. In a small bowl, whisk together the soy sauce, cornstarch, brown sugar, water, salt and pepper until well combined.

6. Add the soy sauce mixture to the pan with the garlic and ginger and stir to combine. Cook for 12 minutes until the sauce has thickened.
7. Add the beef and broccoli back to the pan and stir to coat with the sauce. Cook for an additional 12 minutes until everything is heated through.
8. Serve immediately over rice or noodles, if desired.
9. Enjoy your delicious beef and broccoli stir fry!

Balsamic Glaze

Ingredients:

- 1 cup balsamic vinegar
- 2 tablespoons honey or maple syrup (optional)

Directions:

1. Pour the balsamic vinegar into a small saucepan.
2. If desired, add honey or maple syrup for a touch of sweetness.
3. Bring the mixture to a boil over medium high heat, then reduce the heat to low.
4. Simmer for about 1520 minutes until the balsamic vinegar has thickened and reduced by half, stirring occasionally.
5. Remove from heat and let the balsamic glaze cool for a few minutes.
6. The glaze will thicken further as it cools.

7. Drizzle the balsamic glaze over salads, roasted vegetables, grilled meats, or even fresh fruits for a sweet and tangy flavor.

Almond Butter Cookies

Ingredients:

- 1 egg
- 1 teaspoon vanilla extract
- 1/2 teaspoon baking soda
- Pinch of salt
- 1 cup almond butter
- 1/2 cup coconut sugar or brown sugar
- Optional addins: chocolate chips, chopped nuts, dried fruits

Directions:

1. Preheat the oven to 350°F (175°C) and line a baking sheet with parchment paper.

2. In a bowl, mix together the almond butter, coconut sugar or brown sugar, egg, vanilla extract, baking soda, and salt until well combined.
3. If desired, stir in optional addins such as chocolate chips, chopped nuts, or dried fruits.
4. Scoop tablespoonsized portions of the dough onto the prepared baking sheet, spacing them a few inches apart.
5. Use a fork to gently flatten each cookie and create a crisscross pattern on the top.
6. Bake in the preheated oven for 810 minutes until the edges are lightly golden.
7. Remove from the oven and let the cookies cool on the baking sheet for a few minutes, then transfer them to a wire rack to cool completely.
8. Enjoy the almond butter cookies as a delicious and healthier treat.

Grilled Steak:

Ingredients:

- 2 tablespoons of olive oil
- 2 cloves of garlic
- 1 teaspoon of dried oregano
- 2 steaks
- Salt and pepper to taste

Directions:

1. Preheat your grill to medium heat (or a skillet to medium heat if you don't have a grill).
2. Rub the steaks with the olive oil, garlic, oregano, salt, and pepper.
3. Place the steaks on the preheated grill (or skillet) and cook for 46 minutes per side, or to your desired doneness.

4. Let the steaks rest for a few minutes before serving. Enjoy!

Baked Chicken Breasts

Ingredients:

- 2 cloves of garlic
- 1 teaspoon of dried oregano
- 4 chicken breasts
- 2 tablespoons of olive oil
- salt and pepper to taste

Directions:
1. Preheat oven to 375°F.
2. Rub the chicken breasts with the olive oil, garlic, oregano, salt, and pepper.
3. Place the chicken breasts on a greased baking sheet.
4. Bake in the preheated oven for 2025 minutes, or until chicken is cooked through.

5. Let the chicken rest for a few minutes before serving. Enjoy!

Bacon Wrapped Pork Tenderloin

Ingredients:

- 2 tablespoons of olive oil
- 2 cloves of garlic
- 1 teaspoon of dried oregano
- 1 pork tenderloin
- 68 slices of bacon
- salt and pepper to taste

Directions:
1. Preheat oven to 375°F.
2. Rub the pork tenderloin with the olive oil, garlic, oregano, salt, and pepper.
3. Wrap the pork tenderloin in the bacon slices.
4. Place the pork tenderloin on a greased baking sheet.

5. Bake in the preheated oven for 2530 minutes, or until pork is cooked through.
6. Let the pork rest for a few minutes before serving. Enjoy!

Filet Mignon And Mushroom Eggs Skillet

Ingredients:

- fresh mushrooms (sliced)
- salt and pepper to taste
- Filet mignon steak(s), preferably grass fed and thick cut
- Farm fresh eggs (as many as desired)
- butter or ghee for cooking

Directions:

1. Preheat a castiron skillet over medium high heat. Season the filet mignon steak(s) with salt and pepper on both sides.
2. Add butter or ghee to the skillet and sauté the sliced mushrooms until they are golden and tender. Remove the mushrooms from the skillet and set them aside.

3. In the same skillet, sear the filet mignon steak(s) for approximately 34 minutes on each side, or until they reach your preferred level of doneness.
4. Remove the cooked steak(s) from the skillet and allow them to rest.
5. In the same skillet, crack the farm fresh eggs and cook them to your desired level of doneness, seasoning them with salt and pepper.
6. Arrange the cooked filet mignon steak(s) and sautéed mushrooms in the skillet alongside the eggs.
7. Serve the savory Filet Mignon and Mushroom Eggs Skillet and relish the tender steak and the earthy flavors of mushrooms combined with the luscious eggs.

Sirloin Steak And Vegetable Eggs Skillet

Ingredients:

- Fresh vegetables (e.g., bell peppers, onions, and spinach)
- Salt and pepper to taste
- Sirloin steak(s), preferably grass fed and thick cut
- Farm fresh eggs (as many as desired)
- Butter or ghee for cooking

Directions:
1. Preheat a castiron skillet over medium high heat. Season the sirloin steak(s) with salt and pepper on both sides.
2. Add butter or ghee to the skillet and sauté the fresh vegetables until they are tender and

slightly caramelized. Remove the vegetables from the skillet and set them aside.
3. In the same skillet, sear the sirloin steak(s) for approximately 34 minutes on each side, adjusting the cooking time based on your preferred level of doneness.
4. Remove the cooked steak(s) from the skillet and let them rest.
5. In the same skillet, crack the farm fresh eggs and cook them to your desired level of doneness, seasoning them with salt and pepper.
6. Arrange the cooked sirloin steak(s) and sautéed vegetables in the skillet with the eggs.
7. Serve the delightful Sirloin Steak and Vegetable
8. Eggs Skillet, savoring the delicious combination of tender steak and vibrant vegetables mingling with the luscious eggs.

Roasted Vegetables

Ingredients:

- 2 cups cauliflower florets
- 2 tablespoons olive oil
- 2 cups broccoli florets
- salt and freshly ground black pepper

Directions:

1. Preheat oven to 425 degrees F.
2. Place broccoli and cauliflower on a baking sheet lined with foil.
3. Add salt and chilli & sprinkle with olive oil.
4. Roast in preheated oven for 20 minutes or until vegetables are tender and lightly browned.
5. Serve warm.

Grilled Shrimp

Ingredients:

- 2 tablespoons olive oil
- salt and freshly ground black pepper
- One pound of big shrimp, stripped & deveined

Directions:

1. Preheat grill to high heat.
2. Toss shrimp with olive oil and season with salt and pepper.
3. Grill shrimp for 2 minutes per side or until shrimp are cooked through.
4. Let shrimp rest for 5 minutes before serving.

Baked Cod With Lemon And Herbs

Ingredients:

- 2 tablespoons fresh lemon juice
- 1 teaspoon lemon zest
- 1 teaspoon dried dill
- 1/2 teaspoon dried thyme
- 1/2 teaspoon dried parsley
- 2 cod fillets (6 oz each)
- Salt and pepper to taste
- 1 tablespoon olive oil
- 2 cloves garlic, minced

Directions:

1. Preheat the oven to 400°F (200°C).

2. The cod fillets should be seasoned with salt and pepper on both sides.
3. The fillets should be placed in a clean baking dish.
4. In a small bowl, mix olive oil, lemon juice, lemon zest, dried dill, dried thyme, dried parsley, and minced garlic.
5. Drizzle the lemon and herb mixture over the cod fillets, ensuring they are coated evenly.
6. Bake the cod in the preheated oven for about 1215 minutes until the fish flakes easily with a fork.
7. Serve the cod fillets with the pan juices.

Stuffed Bell Peppers With Ground Beef And Cheese

Ingredients:

- 1 teaspoon dried oregano
- 1 teaspoon dried basil
- 1/2 teaspoon smoked paprika
- 1/4 teaspoon cayenne pepper (optional)
- 1 cup shredded cheddar cheese
- 4 bell peppers (any color)
- 1 lb ground beef
- 1/2 cup chopped onion
- 2 cloves garlic, minced
- salt and pepper to taste

- fresh parsley, chopped (for garnish)

Directions:

1. Preheat the oven to 375°F (190°C).
2. Bell peppers' tops should be cut off, and the seeds and membranes should be removed.
3. In a skillet, cook the ground beef, chopped onion, and minced garlic over medium heat until the beef is browned and the onion is translucent. Drain any excess grease.
4. Season the beef mixture with salt, pepper, dried oregano, dried basil, smoked paprika, and cayenne pepper (if using).
5. Fill the bell peppers with the seasoned ground beef mixture and place them in a baking dish.
6. Bake the stuffed bell peppers in the preheated oven for about 2530 minutes until the peppers are tender and the filling is cooked through.
7. Sprinkle shredded cheddar cheese over the tops of the bell peppers and return them to

the oven for an additional 5 minutes until the cheese is melted and bubbly.
8. Garnish with fresh chopped parsley before serving.

Bacon Wrapped Pork Chops

Ingredients:

- Pork chops
- bacon slices
- salt and pepper to taste

Directions:

1. Preheat the oven to 400°F (200°C).
2. Season the pork chops with salt and pepper.
3. Wrap a slice of bacon around each pork chop.
4. Place the bacon wrapped pork chops on a baking sheet lined with parchment paper.
5. Bake in the preheated oven for about 2530 minutes or until the pork chops are cooked through and the bacon is crispy.
6. Remove from the oven and let them rest for a few minutes before serving.

Beef Jerky:

Ingredients:

- 1 pound of lean beef (such as eye of round or top round)
- salt and pepper to taste
- optional: garlic powder, onion powder, smoked paprika for additional flavor

Directions:
1. Slice the beef into thin strips, about ¼ inch thick.
2. Season the beef strips with salt, pepper, and any additional spices you prefer.
3. Place the seasoned beef strips on a baking sheet lined with parchment paper.
4. Bake in a low temperature oven (around 175°F or 80°C) for 24 hours until the beef is dried and chewy.

5. Allow the beef jerky to cool completely before storing in an airtight container.

Delicious Beef Tacos

Ingredients:

- 2 tbsp. Butter, melted
- 1 cup chicken stock
- 1 tsp. Garlic, minced
- 2 lb. Round roast, cut into chunks
- 1 tsp. Salt

Directions:

1. Heat butter in a pan over medium heat.
2. Add meat and cook until browned from all the sides.
3. Transfer meat to the slow cooker.
4. Pour remaining Ingredients: over meat.
5. Cover and cook on high for 6 hours.
6. Shred the meat using a fork and serve.

Mustard Chuck Roast

Ingredients:

- 1 tsp. Garlic powder

- 2 1/2 tbsp. Yellow mustard

- 4 oz. Heavy cream

- 3 lb. Beef chuck roast, cut into 1inch cubes

- 1 tsp. Salt

Directions:
1. Add heavy cream, garlic powder, mustard, and salt into the slow cooker and stir well.
2. Add meat and stir to coat.
3. Cover and cook on low for 6 hours.
4. Serve and enjoy.

Sandwich Recipe

Ingredients:

- 1 egg
- 1 ounce cheddar cheese
- 2 sausage patties beef used in picture and for calculations
- 1 teaspoon butter or bacon grease, if you have it

Directions:
1. In a large skillet, melt butter over medium heat.
2. Form sausage into thin patties, about the size of your palm but only 1/2 inch thick.
3. Cook patties until they brown on one side, then flip, cooking for another 23 minutes, or until cooked through.

4. If you don't mind your food touching, fry an egg at the same time in the same pan.
5. If not, you can use a little more butter in an additional pan (medium heat, and wait until the pan is hot to prevent sticking), and then assemble your carnivore breakfast sandwich. Keep the yolk runny, as your sauce.
6. To assemble, place one sausage patty on a plate, then top with fried egg, slice of cheese, and another sausage patty.
7. Enjoy!
8. Sliced avocado, tomato, or sauteed spinach can be added as well.

Korean Steamed Egg With Machaca Recipe

Ingredients:

- 2 tsp fish sauce

- Optional: salt & pepper to taste

- Optional: green onion for garnish

- 1 cup stock of choice

- 4 large eggs

- ¼ cup carne seca machaca

Directions:
1. Add 1 Cup stock to the pot and set over medium heat.
2. Crack 4 eggs into liquid measuring cup and whisk until mixed

3. Add ¼ cup Carne Seca Machaca, 2 Tsp Fish Sauce, and salt/pepper (if using) to eggs and mix to incorporate.
4. Once stock comes to a low boil, add egg mixture, whisk to incorporate, cover, and lower heat to medium low.
5. Cook covered on mediumlow heat for 6 minutes.
6. Turn off heat, remove the lid, and allow the Machaca steamed egg mixture to cool down.
7. ENJOY! :)

Breakfast Tacos Recipe

Ingredients:

- Reserved bacon fat (2 tbsp)
- 1 oz. People's choice machaca
- 4 eggs
- 8 strips of bacon, cut in half
- Optional: salt and cheddar cheese

Directions:
1. Bacon weave tortilla
2. Preheat oven to 400 degrees Fahrenheit
3. Lay 4 half strips of bacon down side by side on a lined baking sheet
4. Fold every other piece of bacon up and over itself

5. Lay one piece of bacon down on top (crosswise), then fold the other bacon strips back down to create a weave.
6. Continue with the rest of the bacon until the bacon weave "tortilla" is complete
7. Repeat steps with the remaining halfstrips of bacon to create your second bacon tortilla
8. Place a cookie sheet upside down and onto the bacon weave tortillas. This will prevent the bacon from curling up while cooking
9. Bake in a 400degree oven for 2530 mins
10. Remove, and let your bacon weave tortilla cool
11. Reserve all bacon fat for the next steps

Tasty Chuck Roast

Ingredients:

- 1/2 cup beef broth

- 25 garlic cloves, peeled

- 2 lbs. Beef chuck roast

- 2 tbsp. Vinegar

Directions:

1. Place meat into the slow cooker.
2. Pour remaining Ingredients:over meat.
3. Cover and cook on low for 10 hours.
4. Remove meat from slow cooker and shred using a fork.
5. Return shredded meat to the slow cooker and stir well.
6. Serve and enjoy.

Savory Shredded Beef

Ingredients:

- 2 tbsp. Butter, melted
- 1 tbsp. Balsamic vinegar
- 1 tsp. Oregano
- 1 tsp. Thyme
- 1 tbsp. Garlic, minced
- 1 lb. Beef chuck roast
- 1 cup beef broth
- Pepper
- Salt

Directions:

1. Add butter into the instant pot and set the pot on sauté mode.

2. Add garlic and sauté for a minute.
3. Add meat and sear for 2 minutes.
4. Season with thyme, oregano, pepper, and salt.
5. Add balsamic vinegar and broth and then stir well.
6. Secure pot with lid and cook on high for 30 minutes.
7. Once done, allow to release pressure naturally then remove the lid.
8. Shred the meat using a fork.
9. Serve and enjoy.

Meatballs

Ingredients:

- 1 tsp. Oregano
- 1 tsp. Cinnamon
- 1 tsp. Garlic, minced
- 1/4 tsp. Pepper
- 2 lb. Ground beef
- 1 egg, lightly beaten
- 1/2 tsp. Allspice
- 1/2 tsp. Salt

Directions:
1. Preheat the oven to 400 F.
2. Add all Ingredients:into the large mixing bowl and mix until well combined.

3. Make small balls from the meat mixture and place onto the baking tray.
4. Bake for 1520 minutes.
5. Serve and enjoy.

Pizza

Ingredients:

- 1/4 cup cooked and crumbled bacon
- 1/4 cup sliced pepperoni
- 1/4 cup cooked and crumbled sausage
- 1 lowcarb pizza crust
- 1/2 cup sugar free tomato sauce
- 1/2 cup shredded mozzarella cheese
- Salt and pepper

Directions:
1. Pre heat oven to a temperature of 425°F.
2. Put pizza crust on baking sheet.
3. Spread tomato sauce on crust, you can leave border around edges.
4. You can sprinkle shredded cheese over sauce.

5. Put pepperoni, sausage and cooked bacon on top of cheese.
6. You can season using salt and pepper.
7. You can bake in oven for about 12 minutes.
8. You can begin to slice the pizza then serve as it is hot.
9. Description: This recipe is a good way for you to enjoy delicious meal.

Sausage And Scrambled Eggs

Ingredients:

- 2 breakfast sausages, that is sliced
- Salt and pepper
- 2 eggs
- Olive oil for cooking

Directions:

1. Using a small bowl beat egg and season using salt and pepper.
2. Heat nonstick pan on medium heat then add tablespoon of olive oil. Put your slice sausage then cook for about 3 minutes until you notice that it begin to brown.
3. Pour beaten egg into pan, scramble the egg mixture with sausage using spatula. Cook for about 3 minutes until you notice that the eggs are set.

4. You can begin to serve and serve when it is hot.
5. Description: This meal is easy to prepare, it is a good meal for carnivore diet. You will fill full when you eat this meal.

Casserole

Ingredients:

- 1/2 cup of sour cream
- 1 cup of shredded cheddar cheese
- 1/2 cup of chopped onion
- 1/2 cup of chopped green pepper
- 1/2 cup of chopped mushrooms
- 2 garlic cloves, minced
- 2 tbsp of butter
- 1 lb of ground beef
- 1 lb of ground pork
- 1/2 cup of beef broth
- 1/2 cup of heavy cream

- Salt and pepper

Directions:

1. Preheat oven to a temperature of 350°F
2. Heat skillet on medium high heat then put pork and ground beef. Cook until it becomes brown and stir occasionally.
3. Drain excess fat from skillet you can transfer meat to casserole dish.
4. Using same skillet melt butter on medium heat. Put green pepper, chopped onion, garlic, and mushroom. Cook till it become soft and stir occasionally.
5. Pour cook vegetable over meat on casserole dish.
6. In another bowl whisk beef broth, sour cream and heavy cream. You can pour this mixture on the vegetable and meat in casserole dish.
7. Sprinkle shredded cheddar cheese on top.
8. Bake in oven for close to 30 minutes.
9. You can serve when hot.

10. Description: This is a very good way to enjoy casserole meal as you practice carnivore diet.

Stuffed Portobello Mushrooms With Ground Beef And Cheese

Ingredients:

- 2 cloves garlic, minced
- salt and pepper to taste
- 1 teaspoon dried oregano
- 1 teaspoon dried basil
- 1/2 teaspoon smoked paprika
- 1 cup shredded mozzarella cheese
- 4 large portobello mushrooms
- 1 lb ground beef
- 1/2 cup chopped onion
- fresh parsley, chopped (for garnish)

Directions:

1. Preheat the oven to 375°F (190°C).
2. The Portobello mushrooms' stems should be cut off, and a spoon should be used to delicately scrape out the gills.
3. In a skillet, cook the ground beef, chopped onion, and minced garlic over medium heat until the beef is browned and the onion is translucent. Drain any excess grease.
4. Season the beef mixture with salt, pepper, dried oregano, dried basil, and smoked paprika.
5. Spoon the beef mixture into the Portobello mushrooms, dividing it evenly.
6. Place the stuffed mushrooms in a baking dish and bake in the preheated oven for 2025 minutes until the mushrooms are tender and the beef is cooked through.

7. Remove the mushrooms from the oven and sprinkle shredded mozzarella cheese over the tops.
8. Return the mushrooms to the oven for an additional 5 minutes until the cheese is melted and bubbly.
9. Garnish with chopped parsley before serving.

Herbroasted Chicken Thighs

Ingredients:

- 1 teaspoon dried thyme
- 1 teaspoon dried rosemary
- 1 teaspoon dried parsley
- 1/2 teaspoon garlic powder
- 4 chicken thighs, bonein, and skinon
- salt and pepper to taste
- 2 tablespoons olive oil
- 1/2 teaspoon onion powder

Directions:
1. Preheat the oven to 425°F (220°C).
2. The chicken thighs should be seasoned with salt and pepper on both sides.

3. In a small bowl, mix olive oil, dried thyme, dried rosemary, dried parsley, garlic powder, and onion powder to make the herb rub.
4. Rub the herb mixture all over the chicken thighs, coating them evenly.
5. Place the chicken thighs on a lined baking sheet, skin side up.
6. Roast the chicken thighs in the preheated oven for 3035 minutes until they are golden brown and cooked through, with an internal temperature of 165°F (74°C).
7. Remove the chicken thighs from the oven and let them rest for a few minutes before serving.

Classic Baconwrapped Scallops

Ingredients:

- Sea scallops (fresh and large)
- Bacon strips (thinly sliced)
- Toothpicks (for securing the bacon)

Directions:

1. Preheat your oven to 400°F (200°C) to ensure a hot and even cooking environment.
2. Rinse the sea scallops under cold water and pat them dry with paper towels, ensuring they are moisturefree for a crispy texture.
3. Cut the bacon strips into halves or thirds, depending on the size of the scallops, to ensure they wrap around the seafood beautifully.
4. Wrap each sea scallop with a piece of bacon and secure it in place using a toothpick,

ensuring the bacon encases the scallop securely.
5. Place the baconwrapped scallops on a baking sheet lined with parchment paper or a wire rack to ensure even cooking and prevent sticking.
6. Bake the baconwrapped scallops in the preheated oven for approximately 1215 minutes, or until the bacon becomes crispy and the scallops are cooked through and tender.
7. Once the baconwrapped scallops are cooked to perfection, remove the toothpicks before serving to reveal the beautiful and mouthwatering appetizers.
8. Serve the classic baconwrapped scallops as an exquisite and proteinrich appetizer or main course, capturing the essence of indulgence and satisfaction in each delightful bite.

Garlicherb Baconwrapped Scallops

Ingredients:

- Toothpicks (for securing the bacon)
- Fresh garlic (minced)
- Fresh rosemary leaves (chopped)
- Fresh thyme leaves (chopped)
- Sea scallops (fresh and large)
- Bacon strips (thinly sliced)
- Salt and pepper to taste

Directions:
1. Prepare the sea scallops by rinsing them under cold water and patting them dry with paper towels to remove excess moisture.
2. In a small bowl, combine minced fresh garlic, chopped fresh rosemary, chopped fresh

thyme, salt, and pepper to create a flavorful herb mixture.
3. Wrap each sea scallop with a piece of bacon, then sprinkle the herb mixture over the baconwrapped scallops, ensuring the herbs adhere to the bacon.
4. Secure the bacon in place with toothpicks, making sure the herbinfused bacon encases the scallops snugly.
5. Place the garlicherb baconwrapped scallops on a baking sheet lined with parchment paper or a wire rack for even cooking and easy cleanup.
6. Bake the garlicherb baconwrapped scallops in the preheated oven at 400°F (200°C) for approximately 1215 minutes, or until the bacon is crispy and the scallops are cooked through and tender.
7. Once the baconwrapped scallops are cooked to perfection, remove the toothpicks before

serving, unveiling the aromatic and delectable appetizers.

8. Serve the garlicherb baconwrapped scallops as an exquisite and flavorful appetizer or main course, celebrating the harmonious marriage of herbs, garlic, and savory bacon with the delicate sweetness of the sea scallops.

Mapleglazed Baconwrapped Scallops

Ingredients:

- Toothpicks (for securing the bacon)
- Maple syrup (pure and unsweetened)
- Dijon mustard
- Sea scallops (fresh and large)
- Bacon strips (thinly sliced)
- Salt and pepper to taste

Directions:

1. Begin by rinsing the sea scallops under cold water and patting them dry with paper towels to ensure a dry surface.
2. In a small bowl, combine pure maple syrup and Dijon mustard to create a luscious and tangy glaze for the baconwrapped scallops.

3. Wrap each sea scallop with a piece of bacon, then brush the mapleDijon glaze over the baconwrapped scallops, ensuring they are coated evenly.
4. Secure the bacon in place with toothpicks, allowing the mapleDijon glazed bacon to envelop the scallops enticingly.
5. Place the mapleglazed baconwrapped scallops on a baking sheet lined with parchment paper or a wire rack to avoid sticking and promote even cooking.
6. Bake the mapleglazed baconwrapped scallops in the preheated oven at 400°F (200°C) for approximately 1215 minutes, or until the bacon becomes crispy and the scallops are cooked through and tender.
7. Once the baconwrapped scallops are cooked to perfection, remove the toothpicks before serving to unveil the delectable and mapleinfused appetizers.

8. Serve the mapleglazed baconwrapped scallops as an exquisite and sweetsavory appetizer or main course, harmonizing the delightful flavors of maple, Dijon, and succulent scallops in a divine culinary symphony.

Banana Cake

Ingredients:

- 1/2 teaspoon baking soda
- 1/4 teaspoon salt
- 2 bananas, mashed
- 1/4 cup coconut oil, melted
- 1 cup almond flour
- 1/4 cup coconut sugar
- 1 teaspoon baking powder
- 1 teaspoon vanilla extract

Directions:

1. Preheat oven to 350F and grease an 8inch round cake pan.

2. In a medium bowl, mix together almond flour, coconut sugar, baking powder, baking soda, and salt.
3. In a separate bowl, mix together mashed bananas, coconut oil, and vanilla extract.
4. Pour wet Ingredients:into dry Ingredients:and mix until combined.
5. Pour batter into cake pan and spread evenly.
6. Bake for 2530 minutes until a toothpick inserted in the center comes out clean.
7. Remove from oven and let cool before serving.

Salted Caramel Apple Tart

Ingredients:

- 3 tablespoons coconut oil, melted
- 2 apples, thinly sliced
- 2 tablespoons maple syrup
- 1 teaspoon ground cinnamon
- 1/2 cup almond flour
- 1/4 cup coconut sugar
- 1/4 teaspoon salt
- 1/4 cup salted caramel sauce

Directions:

1. Preheat oven to 350F and grease an 8 or 9inch tart pan.

2. In a medium bowl, mix together almond flour, coconut sugar, and salt.
3. Add in melted coconut oil and mix until combined.
4. Press dough into tart pan and bake for 10 minutes.
5. Meanwhile, in a medium bowl, mix together apples, maple syrup, and ground cinnamon.
6. Remove tart pan from oven and spread salted caramel sauce on top.
7. Arrange apple slices on top and bake for 20-25 minutes until golden brown.
8. Remove from oven and let cool before serving.

Chocolate Peanut Butter Pie:

Ingredients:

- 1/4 teaspoon salt
- 1/4 cup dark chocolate chips
- 1/4 cup natural peanut butter
- 1/4 cup coconut milk
- 1/4 cup maple syrup
- 1/2 cup almond flour
- 2 tablespoons coconut oil, melted
- 1 teaspoon vanilla extract

Directions:

1. Preheat oven to 350F and grease an 8inch tart pan.

2. In a medium bowl, mix together almond flour, melted coconut oil, and salt.
3. Press dough into tart pan and bake for 10 minutes.
4. Meanwhile, in a medium saucepan over low heat, melt together dark chocolate chips, peanut butter, coconut milk, maple syrup, and vanilla extract.
5. Remove tart pan from oven and spread melted chocolate mixture on top.
6. Bake for 1520 minutes until set.
7. Remove from oven and let cool before serving.

Chimichurri Sauce

Ingredients:

- 1/4 cup red wine vinegar
- 1/2 cup olive oil
- 1 teaspoon dried oregano
- 1/2 teaspoon red pepper flakes (optional)
- 1 cup fresh parsley, chopped
- 1/4 cup fresh cilantro, chopped
- 3 cloves garlic, minced
- salt and pepper to taste

Directions:

1. In a bowl, combine the chopped parsley, cilantro, minced garlic, red wine vinegar, olive

oil, dried oregano, red pepper flakes (if desired), salt, and pepper.
2. Stir well to mix all the Ingredients:together.
3. Let the chimichurri sauce sit at room temperature for at least 15 minutes to allow the flavors to meld.
4. Adjust the seasoning if needed.
5. Serve the chimichurri sauce as a flavorful accompaniment to grilled meats or roasted vegetables.

Homemade Ranch Dressing

Ingredients:

- 1 tablespoon fresh chives, chopped
- 1 tablespoon fresh parsley, chopped
- 1 clove garlic, minced
- 1/2 teaspoon dried dill
- 1/2 teaspoon onion powder
- 1/2 cup mayonnaise
- 1/2 cup sour cream or greek yogurt
- 1/4 cup buttermilk
- salt and pepper to taste

Directions:

1. In a bowl, whisk together the mayonnaise, sour cream or Greek yogurt, buttermilk, chopped chives, chopped parsley, minced garlic, dried dill, onion powder, salt, and pepper until well combined.
2. Taste and adjust the seasoning if needed.
3. Refrigerate the ranch dressing for at least 30 minutes to allow the flavors to meld.
4. Serve the homemade ranch dressing as a versatile condiment for salads, veggies, or as a dipping sauce.

Spicy Mustard Sauce

Ingredients:

- 1 tablespoon hot sauce (such as sriracha or tabasco)
- 1 tablespoon honey
- 1 teaspoon apple cider vinegar
- 1/4 cup dijon mustard
- 1 tablespoon mayonnaise
- salt and pepper to taste

Directions:

1. In a small bowl, whisk together the Dijon mustard, mayonnaise, hot sauce, honey, apple cider vinegar, salt, and pepper until smooth and well combined.
2. Taste and adjust the seasoning if needed.

3. Let the spicy mustard sauce sit at room temperature for a few minutes to allow the flavors to meld.
4. Serve the spicy mustard sauce as a zesty and tangy accompaniment to sandwiches, grilled meats, or roasted vegetables.

Bacon Wrapped Shrimp With Spicy Mayo Dipping Sauce

Ingredients:

- 1/2 cup mayonnaise
- 2 tbsp hot sauce
- 1 tsp paprika
- 1 lb large shrimp, peeled and deveined
- 12 slices of bacon
- Salt and pepper, to taste

Directions:

1. Preheat the oven to 400°F (200°C).
2. In a small bowl, mix together the mayonnaise, hot sauce, paprika, and salt and pepper to create the spicy mayo dipping sauce. Set aside.

3. Take a slice of bacon and wrap it around a shrimp, securing it with a toothpick. Repeat until all shrimp are wrapped.
4. Place the bacon wrapped shrimp on a baking sheet and bake for 1215 minutes, or until the bacon is crispy and the shrimp is cooked through.
5. Serve the bacon wrapped shrimp hot with the spicy mayo dipping sauce on the side.
6. Enjoy your delicious bacon wrapped shrimp with spicy mayo dipping sauce as a satisfying and proteinpacked dish for your carnivore diet cookbook!

Grilled Salmon With Lemon And Herb Butter

Ingredients:

- 2 tablespoons fresh parsley, chopped
- 2 tablespoons fresh chives, chopped
- 2 tablespoons fresh dill, chopped
- 1 clove garlic, minced
- Salt and pepper, to taste
- 4 salmon filets
- 1/2 cup butter, softened
- 1 lemon, cut into wedges

Directions:

1. Preheat your grill to medium high heat.

2. In a small bowl, combine the softened butter, chopped parsley, chives, dill, minced garlic, salt, and pepper. Mix well to combine.
3. Place the salmon filets on a large piece of aluminum foil. Season the filets with salt and pepper.
4. Spread a generous amount of the herb butter over each filet.
5. Fold the foil over the salmon, sealing the edges to create a packet.
6. Place the salmon packets on the grill and cook for about 1012 minutes, or until the salmon is cooked through and flaky.
7. Carefully remove the salmon packets from the grill and open them up.
8. Serve the salmon filets with lemon wedges on the side. Squeeze the lemon over the salmon just before eating for an extra burst of flavor.
9. Enjoy your delicious and healthy grilled salmon with lemon and herb butter!

Stuffed Mushrooms

Ingredients:

- 1/4 cup grated parmesan cheese
- 1 tablespoon chopped fresh parsley
- 1 garlic clove, minced
- 12 large button mushrooms
- 4 oz cream cheese, softened
- Salt and pepper to taste

Directions:

1. Preheat your oven to 375°F (190°C) and line a baking sheet with parchment paper.
2. Remove the stems from the mushrooms and hollow out the centers slightly to create space for the filling.

3. In a bowl, mix the softened cream cheese, grated Parmesan cheese, chopped fresh parsley, minced garlic, salt, and pepper until well combined.
4. Stuff each mushroom cap with the cream cheese mixture, pressing it down gently.
5. Place the stuffed mushrooms on the prepared baking sheet.
6. Bake in the preheated oven for 1520 minutes or until the mushrooms are tender and the filling is lightly browned and bubbly.
7. Serve the Stuffed Mushrooms hot and enjoy the delightful combination of flavors!

Zucchini Noodles

Ingredients:

- 2 large zucchinis
- 2 tablespoons olive oil
- 2 garlic cloves, minced
- Salt and pepper to taste

Directions:

1. Wash the zucchinis and trim the ends.
2. Using a spiralizer or a vegetable peeler, create zucchini noodles by slicing the zucchinis lengthwise into thin ribbons.
3. In a skillet over medium heat, heat the olive oil.
4. Add the minced garlic to the skillet and sauté it for a minute until fragrant.

5. Add the zucchini noodles to the skillet and sauté them for 23 minutes or until they are tender crisp.
6. Season the Zucchini Noodles with salt and pepper to taste.
7. Serve the zucchini noodles as a nutritious and low carb alternative to pasta.

Keto Chocolate Mousse

Ingredients:

- 1/4 cup powdered erythritol (or any other lowcarb sweetener)
- 1 teaspoon vanilla extract
- 1 cup heavy cream
- 1/4 cup unsweetened cocoa powder

Directions:

1. In a mixing bowl, combine the heavy cream, unsweetened cocoa powder, powdered erythritol, and vanilla extract.
2. Use an electric mixer to beat the mixture until it forms stiff peaks.
3. Divide the Keto Chocolate Mousse among serving cups or bowls.
4. Refrigerate the mousse for at least 1 hour before serving.

5. Garnish with shaved dark chocolate or whipped cream if desired. Enjoy this rich and indulgent dessert!

Spaghetti Carbonara

Ingredients:

- 200 g guanciale or bacon
- Smoked, cut into cubes
- 4 egg yolks, 100 g pecorino cheese
- Grated roman, salt to taste
- 400 g spaghetti
- Freshly ground black pepper to taste.

Directions:

1. Start by bringing a pot of salted water to a boil. Cook the spaghetti according to the Directions: on the package until al dente.
2. Meanwhile, in a large skillet, brown the cubes of guanciale or pancetta over medium high heat until golden brown and crispy.

3. Remove the skillet from the heat. In a bowl, whisk the egg yolks with the grated pecorino Romano cheese.
4. Add a generous grinding of black pepper and mix well. Drain the spaghetti al dente, reserving some of the cooking water.
5. Add the spaghetti to the skillet with the guanciale or pancetta and stir well to allow the meat fat to flavor. Remove the skillet from the heat and add the egg and cheese mixture, stirring vigorously to combine the ingredients.
6. Add a little spaghetti cooking water if the pasta is too dry. Make sure the eggandcheese sauce has thickened and envelops the spaghetti well.
7. Serve the spaghetti carbonara hot, garnished with a sprinkling of grated pecorino Romano cheese and freshly ground black pepper.

Lasagna Bolognese

Ingredients:

- 2 cloves of garlic, finely chopped
- 400 g tomato pulp
- 2 tablespoons of tomato paste
- 1/2 cup of red wine
- 1 cup of milk
- 1/2 cup meat stock
- 50 g butter, 50 g flour
- 200 g grated parmesan cheese
- 12 sheets of lasagna noodles
- 500 g minced meat
- Onion, finely chopped
- Salt and pepper to taste

- Nutmeg to taste.

Directions:

1. Start by preparing the Bolognese sauce. In a large skillet, sauté the onion and garlic in a little olive oil until translucent.
2. Add the ground meat to the skillet and cook until well browned and free of liquid. Add the tomato pulp, tomato paste and red wine.
3. Stir well and cook over medium low heat for about 1520 minutes, until the ragout has thickened. Add the milk and meat stock to the meat sauce.
4. Stir well and let it cook for another 10 minutes. Adjust salt, pepper and nutmeg to taste. Keep the Bolognese sauce aside. In a separate pot, prepare the béchamel sauce.

Pizza

Ingredients:

For the Carnivore Pizza Crust:

- 1 tbsp grassfed ghee (or butter)
- 1 tbsp italian seasoning (optional)
- 1/4 tsp sea salt
- 1 lb ground chicken (or ground meat of your choice)
- 3 eggs
- 5 oz pork rinds

For the carnivore pizza:

- 1 lb ground pork
- 810 slices pepperoni
- 1 tbsp italian seasoning

- 1 block raw cheese

- 10 pieces bacon

- Sea salt (to taste)

Directions:

1. While the crust is baking, prepare the toppings. Start by making the bacon.
2. Chop up the bacon into thin slivers (like 1/4 inch x 1 inch).
3. At medium heat, cook the bacon.
4. Once the bacon is cooked to your liking, remove it from the pan and place it on a plate to cool.
5. Make the sausage.
6. Add the ground pork to the pan with the bacon fat and increase to mediumhigh heat.
7. Add the Italian seasoning (if using) and salt to taste.

8. Cook the ground pork in the bacon fat until browned. Your goal is a nice, deep brown char. This usually takes 1015 minutes.
9. Once the sausage is cooked to your liking, remove it from heat and leave it to cool.
10. Once the Carnivore Pizza Crust is finished baking, add the toppings to the pizza.
11. Grate the block of raw cheese over the body of the pizza crust to form a thick layer.
12. On top of the cheese, add the cooked sausage and bacon.
13. Garnish with pepperoni.
14. Bake the pizza (with the toppings) at 350 degrees for 1015 minutes.
15. Once the toppings have melted and set, remove the pizza from the oven.
16. Let it cool for 1015 minutes, then serve and devour!

17. This pizza is best served fresh, although it will last in the fridge for 34 days in an airtight container.

Steak Nuggets With Chipotle Ranch Dip

Ingredients:

- 1/2 cup grated parmesan cheese

- 1/2 cup pork panko

- 1/2 teaspoon homemade seasoned salt

- 1 pound venison steak or beef steak, cut into chunks.

- 1 large egg(s), organic pasture raised

- Lard or palm oil for frying

- Keto breading

Chipotle ranch dip

- 1/4 cup mayonnaise

- 1/4 cup sour cream (organic, cultured)

- 1+ teaspoon chipotle paste to taste

- 1/2 teaspoon homemade ranch dressing & dip mix

- 1/4 medium lime, juiced

Directions:

1. For the Chipotle Ranch Dip: Combine all ingredients, mix well. 1 teaspoon of chipotle paste yields a mediumspice version, use more or less according to your own taste preferences. I encourage you to use my homemade ranch dressing and dip mix, it's superior to any store brought version. Refrigerate at least 30 minutes before serving, will keep for up to 1 week.
2. Combine Pork Panko, parmesan cheese and seasoned salt again use my homemade not the store bought stuff. Set aside.
3. Beat 1 egg.. place beaten egg 1 bowl and breading mix in another.

4. Dip chunks of steak in egg, then breading. Place on a wax paper lined sheet pan or plate.
5. FREEZE breaded raw steak bites for 30 minutes before frying. This helps to ensure that the breading will NOT LIFT when fried.
6. Heat Lard to roughly 325 degrees F. Working in batches as necessary, fry steak nuggets (from frozen or chilled) until browned, about 23 minutes.
7. Transfer to a papertowel lined plate, season with a sprinkle of salt and serve with Chipotle Ranch.

Cheesy Air Fryer Meatballs Recipe – Keto & Carnivore

Ingredients:

- 2 ounces pork rinds
- 3 ounces shredded italian cheese blend
- 1 tsp pink sea salt
- 2 pounds grassfed ground beef
- 2 large pastured eggs
- 1 tbsp lard

Directions:

1. Place all ingredients in a mixing bowl. With clean hands, knead the mixture until thoroughly combined.
2. Air Fryer Meatball Recipe for a Keto Diet.

3. Roll into balls approximately 1 ½ inches in diameter. This should make 24 meatballs.
4. Air Fryer Meatball Recipe for a Keto Diet. ~Angela of @AdvantageMeals #ketoRecipe
5. Depending on the size of your air fryer, you'll cook them in batches.
6. Line your fryer basket with liners, if you use them. Otherwise, spray with cooking spray.
7. Place meatballs in the basket, making sure they do not touch each other or the sides of the basket.
8. Cook at 350 degrees for 8 minutes. Pull out the basket and turn the meat balls over. Return to fryer and cook at 350 degrees for another 4 minutes.
9. Meatballs should reach an internal temperature of 165 degrees, and then they're done!

Beef Stew Meat

Ingredients:

- 2 tbsp. Vinegar
- 2 garlic cloves
- 1 tbsp. Butter, melted
- 1/2 tsp. Pepper
- 3 lb. Beef stew meat
- 1 tbsp. Dried oregano
- 1/2 cup beef broth
- 3/4 tsp. Salt

Directions:
1. Add butter into the instant pot and set the pot on sauté mode.
2. Add meat to the pot and sauté until browned.

3. Add remaining Ingredients: and stir well.
4. Secure pot with lid and cook on high for 30 minutes.
5. Once done then allow to release pressure naturally then remove the lid.
6. Shred the meat using a fork and stir well.
7. Serve and enjoy.

Steak Bites

Ingredients:

- 1/4 tsp. Pepper
- 1 cup beef stock
- 1/2 tsp. Salt
- 2 3/4 lb. Round steak, cut into bites
- 2 garlic cloves, minced
- 1/4 cup butter, melted

Directions:
1. Add all Ingredients: to the instant pot and stir well.
2. Secure pot with lid and cook on high for 20 minutes.

3. Once done then release pressure using the quick release then remove the lid. Stir well and serve.

Tasty Flank Steak

Ingredients:

- 1 1/2 tsp. Paprika
- 2 tbsp. Butter, melted
- 3 garlic cloves, minced
- 1/2 cup chicken stock
- 1 1/2 lb. Flank steak, cut into strips
- 1/4 tsp. Oregano
- Pepper
- Salt

Directions:
1. Season meat with pepper and salt.
2. Add butter into the instant pot and set the pot on sauté mode.

3. Add meat and sauté until brown.
4. Add remaining Ingredients: and stir to combine.
5. Secure pot with lid and cook on high for 15 minutes.
6. Once done then allow to release pressure naturally then remove the lid.
7. Shred the meat using a fork and serve.

STEAK AND VEGGIES

Ingredients:

- 1 cup of your spinach leaves
- Salt and pepper to taste
- Olive oil for cooking
- 1 steak
- 1 cup of your sliced mushrooms

Directions:

1. Heat grill pan on medium heat, rub steak using olive oil then season using salt and pepper.
2. Grill steak for close to 4 to 5 minutes for each side or you can do it till you get you require level of doneness.
3. On another pan, heat tablespoon of olive oil on a medium heat. Add sliced of mushroom

then cook it until it begin to soften for about 5 minutes.
4. You can add spinach leaves to pan then cook for close to 3 minutes, until you notice that the spinach becomes wilted.
5. Serve steak using sautéed mushrooms with spinach on side.

Sausage And Cheese Omelet

Ingredients:

- 1/4 cup of shredded cheese

- Salt and pepper to taste

- 2 eggs

- 2 cooked sausages, that is sliced

- Olive oil for cooking

Directions:

1. Beat eggs on a bowl then season using salt and pepper.
2. Heat nonstick pan on a medium heat then add tablespoon of olive oil. Put sliced sausage then cook for close to 3 minutes, until you notice that they have begun to brown.
3. Pour beaten eggs into pan and allow it to cook for 3 minutes.

4. Sprinkle shredded cheese over eggs then make use of spatula in folding the omelet in half. You can cook for another 3 minutes until you notice that the cheese is melted.
5. You can begin to serve the omelet do this when the omelet is hot.
6. Description: This is a good breakfast for you to start your day. The cheese and sausage give the egg richness and flavor.

Salmon And Avocado

Ingredients:

- 1/2 avocado, sliced
- 1/2 lemon, juiced
- 2 slices of smoked salmon
- Salt and pepper to taste

Directions:

1. Place smoked salmon on your plate.
2. Then you can slice avocado in half then you can remove the pit. You can begin to slice the avocado into thin slices.
3. Then put the thin slice avocado on your smoked salmon
4. Squeeze lemon juice on salmon and avocado
5. You can season using salt and pepper.
6. You can serve the dish.

7. Description: This meal is good for those who want light meal. The salmon is a good source of healthy fats and protein. The avocado provides fiber for the body.

Greek Style Grilled Lamb Chops

Ingredients:

- 2 cloves garlic, minced
- 1 teaspoon dried oregano
- 1/2 teaspoon dried thyme
- 1/2 teaspoon dried rosemary
- 1/2 teaspoon smoked paprika
- 8 lamb chops (about 2 lbs)
- salt and pepper to taste
- 2 tablespoons olive oil
- 2 tablespoons fresh lemon juice
- fresh mint leaves (for garnish)

Directions:

1. Preheat the grill to medium high heat.
2. The lamb chops should be seasoned with salt and pepper on both sides.
3. In a small bowl, whisk together olive oil, lemon juice, minced garlic, dried oregano, dried thyme, dried rosemary, and smoked paprika to make the marinade.
4. Place the lamb chops in a shallow dish and pour the marinade over them. Flip the chops to coat them evenly.
5. Let the lamb chops marinate for at least 30 minutes, or refrigerate them for up to 4 hours for more flavor.
6. Remove the lamb chops from the marinade and discard the excess marinade.
7. Grill the lamb chops for about 34 minutes per side until they are cooked to your desired level of doneness.
8. Remove the lamb chops from the grill and let them rest for a few minutes before serving.

9. Garnish with fresh mint leaves before serving.

Baked Lemon Herb Salmon

Ingredients:

- 2 tablespoons fresh lemon juice
- 1 teaspoon lemon zest
- 1 teaspoon dried dill
- 1 teaspoon dried parsley
- 2 salmon fillets (6 oz each)
- salt and pepper to taste
- 2 tablespoons olive oil
- 1/2 teaspoon garlic powder

Directions:
1. Preheat the oven to 400°F (200°C).
2. Season the salmon fillets with salt and pepper on both sides.

3. In a small bowl, whisk together olive oil, lemon juice, lemon zest, dried dill, dried parsley, and garlic powder to make the marinade.
4. Place the salmon fillets in a baking dish or on a lined baking sheet.
5. Distribute the marinade evenly over the salmon fillets before serving.
6. Bake the salmon in the preheated oven for 1215 minutes until it flakes easily with a fork.
7. Before serving, take the salmon out of the oven and allow it to rest for a while.

Classic Garlic Butter Mushrooms

Ingredients:

- Grass fed butter (or ghee, for a dairy free option)

- Fresh garlic (minced)

- Salt and pepper to taste

- Fresh mushrooms (such as cremini or button mushrooms)

- Fresh parsley (chopped, for garnish)

Directions:

1. Clean the fresh mushrooms by wiping them with a damp paper towel to remove any dirt or debris.
2. Slice the mushrooms into uniform pieces to ensure even cooking and a pleasing presentation.

3. In a skillet over medium high heat, melt the grass fed butter or ghee.
4. Add the minced fresh garlic to the melted butter and sauté until fragrant, infusing the butter with its aromatic essence.
5. Toss in the sliced mushrooms and sauté them in the garlic butter sauce until they become tender and develop a golden brown color.
6. Season the garlic butter mushrooms with salt and pepper to enhance their flavors.
7. Once the mushrooms are cooked to perfection, transfer them to a serving dish, allowing the garlic butter sauce to coat the mushrooms beautifully.
8. Garnish the dish with chopped fresh parsley for a burst of color and herbal freshness.
9. Serve the classic garlic butter mushrooms as a delightful and nutritious side dish, celebrating the simplicity and richness of this timeless culinary creation.

Lemon Herb Garlic Butter Mushrooms

Ingredients:

- Fresh thyme leaves
- Fresh rosemary leaves
- Lemon zest
- Fresh mushrooms (such as cremini or button mushrooms)
- Grass fed butter (or ghee, for a dairy free option)
- Fresh garlic (minced)
- Salt and pepper to taste

Directions:

1. Clean the fresh mushrooms by wiping them with a damp paper towel to remove any dirt or debris.
2. Slice the mushrooms into uniform pieces for even cooking and an appealing texture.
3. In a skillet over medium high heat, melt the grass fed butter or ghee.
4. Add the minced fresh garlic to the melted butter and sauté until it releases its delightful aroma, infusing the butter with a flavorful base.
5. Stir in the sliced mushrooms, fresh thyme leaves, and fresh rosemary leaves, combining them with the garlic butter sauce to create a herbaceous and aromatic medley.
6. Grate lemon zest over the mushrooms, adding a zesty and vibrant dimension to the dish.
7. Season the lemon herb garlic butter mushrooms with salt and pepper to amplify their taste.

8. Once the mushrooms are tender and infused with the flavors of the garlic butter sauce, transfer them to a serving dish, allowing the herbaceous essence to shine through.
9. Serve the lemon herb garlic butter mushrooms as a refreshing and nutritious side dish, delighting in the harmonious marriage of herbs, lemon, and the earthiness of mushrooms.

Balsamic Glazed Garlic Butter Mushrooms

Ingredients:

- Fresh garlic (minced)
- Balsamic vinegar
- Salt and pepper to taste
- Fresh mushrooms (such as cremini or button mushrooms)
- Grass fed butter (or ghee, for a dairy free option)
- Fresh thyme leaves (optional, for garnish)

Directions:
1. Clean the fresh mushrooms by wiping them with a damp paper towel to ensure they are free from any dirt or debris.

2. Slice the mushrooms into uniform pieces for consistent cooking and a delightful texture.
3. In a skillet over medium high heat, melt the grass fed butter or ghee.
4. Add the minced fresh garlic to the melted butter and sauté until the aroma fills the air, creating a tantalizing garlic butter base.
5. Introduce the sliced mushrooms to the garlic butter sauce, allowing them to cook until they become tender and acquire a golden hue.
6. Pour balsamic vinegar over the mushrooms, adding a delightful tangy and sweet glaze to the dish.
7. Season the balsamic glazed garlic butter mushrooms with salt and pepper to enhance their flavors.
8. Once the mushrooms are coated in the balsamic glaze and infused with the garlic butter sauce, transfer them to a serving dish,

letting the enticing aroma beckon your senses.
9. Garnish the dish with fresh thyme leaves for a touch of herbal fragrance.
10. Serve the balsamic glazed garlic butter mushrooms as a sophisticated and delectable side dish, savoring the interplay of tangy sweetness and savory richness.

Coconut Bacon Bits

Ingredients:

- 2 tablespoons olive oil
- 2 tablespoons tamari
- 1/2 cup coconut flakes
- 1 teaspoon smoked paprika

Directions:

1. Preheat oven to 400F and line a baking sheet with parchment paper.
2. In a medium bowl, mix together coconut flakes, olive oil, tamari, and smoked paprika.
3. Spread mixture onto baking sheet in an even layer.
4. Bake for 1015 minutes until golden brown, stirring every 5 minutes.
5. Remove from oven and let cool before serving.

Coconut Whipped Cream

Ingredients:

- 1 can full fat coconut milk
- 2 tablespoons maple syrup

Directions:

1. Place can of coconut milk in the refrigerator overnight.
2. The next day, open can and scoop out the solid coconut cream from the top, leaving the liquid behind.
3. Place coconut cream in a medium bowl and whip using an electric mixer for 34 minutes.
4. Add in maple syrup and continue to whip for 23 minutes until light and fluffy.
5. Serve chilled.

Coconut Flour Brownies

Ingredients:

- 1/4 teaspoon salt
- 3 tablespoons coconut oil, melted
- 2 eggs
- 1/2 cup coconut flour
- 1/4 cup coconut sugar
- 1/2 teaspoon baking powder
- 1/2 cup dark chocolate chips

Directions:
1. Preheat oven to 350F and grease an 8inch square baking pan.
2. In a medium bowl, mix together coconut flour, coconut sugar, baking powder, and salt.

3. In a separate bowl, mix together melted coconut oil, eggs, and dark chocolate chips.
4. Pour wet Ingredients: into dry Ingredients: and mix until combined.
5. Pour batter into baking pan and spread evenly.
6. Bake for 2025 minutes until a toothpick inserted in the center comes out clean.
7. Remove from oven and let cool before serving.

Baked Sweet Potato Fries

Ingredients:

- 1/2 teaspoon garlic powder
- 1/2 teaspoon onion powder
- Salt and pepper to taste
- 2 large sweet potatoes, cut into fries
- 2 tablespoons olive oil
- 1 teaspoon paprika
- Fresh cilantro or parsley for garnish

Directions:

1. Preheat the oven to 425°F (220°C).
2. In a large bowl, toss the sweet potato fries with olive oil, paprika, garlic powder, onion

powder, salt, and pepper until they are well coated.
3. Spread the sweet potato fries in a single layer on a baking sheet.
4. Bake in the preheated oven for 2530 minutes, flipping them once halfway through, until the fries are crispy and golden brown.
5. Remove from the oven and garnish with fresh cilantro or parsley.
6. Serve the baked sweet potato fries as a healthier alternative to traditional fries.

Lemon Garlic Butter Sauce

Ingredients:

- Juice of 1 lemon
- Zest of 1 lemon
- Salt and pepper to taste
- 4 tablespoons unsalted butter
- 2 cloves garlic, minced
- Chopped fresh parsley for garnish

Directions:
1. Melt the butter in a small saucepan over low heat.
2. Add the minced garlic to the saucepan and sauté for 12 minutes until fragrant.
3. Stir in the lemon juice and lemon zest.
4. Season with salt and pepper to taste.

5. Continue cooking for another minute until the flavors are well combined.
6. Remove from heat and garnish with chopped fresh parsley.
7. Serve the lemon garlic butter sauce as a delicious and tangy drizzle over grilled fish, roasted chicken, or steamed vegetables.

Blackened Salmon Filet

Ingredients:

- 1 tbsp. Of dried thyme
- 1 tbsp. Of dried oregano
- 1 tbsp. Of sea salt
- 1 tsp. Of cayenne pepper
- 2 tbsp. Of butter or ghee
- 2 salmon filets
- 2 tbsp. Of paprika
- 1 tbsp. Of garlic powder
- 1 tbsp. Of onion powder
- Lemon wedges for serving

Directions:

1. Mix all of the dry Ingredients: in a small bowl to create the blackened seasoning.
2. Melt the butter or ghee in a skillet over medium high heat.
3. Coat both sides of each salmon filet with the blackened seasoning, pressing it into the flesh.
4. Place the filets into the hot skillet, skin side up. Cook for about 34 minutes on each side, or until the seasoning has blackened and the salmon is cooked through.
5. Remove the salmon filets from the skillet and serve with lemon wedges on the side.
6. This blackened salmon filet recipe is a delicious and healthy option for a carnivore diet. It's full of flavor and easy to prepare, making it a great addition to any meal plan.

Sizzling Fajitas With Chicken, Steak Or Shrimp

Ingredients:

- 1 tablespoon of olive oil
- 1 teaspoon of chili powder
- 1 teaspoon of paprika
- 1 teaspoon of cumin
- Salt and pepper to taste
- 46 flour tortillas
- 1 pound of chicken, steak or shrimp (peeled and deveined)
- 2 bell peppers (sliced)
- 1 onion (sliced)
- 2 cloves of garlic (minced)
- Lime wedges, guacamole, salsa, and sour cream (optional for serving)

Directions:

1. Heat a large cast-iron skillet over high heat until it's hot.
2. Add the olive oil, sliced onion, and bell peppers to the skillet and stirfry them for 34 minutes, or until the veggies are slightly charred.
3. Add the minced garlic to the skillet and stirfry for another 30 seconds, or until fragrant.
4. Push the veggies to one side of the skillet and add the chicken, steak, or shrimp to the other side. Sprinkle the chili powder, paprika, cumin, salt, and pepper over the meat or seafood.
5. Cook the meat or seafood for 34 minutes, or until browned and cooked through, stirring occasionally.
6. Once the meat or seafood is cooked, combine it with the veggies and stir everything together for another 30 seconds or so.

7. Turn off the heat and let the skillet sit for a minute to cool slightly.
8. Warm the tortillas in a microwave or on a skillet until they're soft and pliable.
9. Serve the sizzling fajitas immediately in the skillet, with the tortillas on the side. Top with lime wedges, guacamole, salsa, and sour cream, if desired.
10. Enjoy your delicious and sizzling fajitas!

BBQ Ribs With Homemade Sauce

Ingredients:

- 2 teaspoons smoked paprika
- 1 teaspoon salt
- 1/2 teaspoon black pepper
- 1 cup beef bone broth
- 1 cup tomato sauce
- 1/2 cup apple cider vinegar
- 1/4 cup honey
- 2 tablespoons worcestershire sauce
- 1 tablespoon dijon mustard
- 2 racks of baby back ribs (approximately 4 pounds)

- 2 teaspoons garlic powder

- 2 teaspoons onion powder

- 1 teaspoon liquid smoke

- 1/2 teaspoon cayenne pepper

Directions:

1. Preheat your oven to 275°F.
2. In a small bowl, combine the garlic powder, onion powder, smoked paprika, salt, and black pepper.
3. Rub the spice mixture all over the ribs, making sure to coat them evenly.
4. Place the ribs on a baking sheet or in a roasting pan, and cover tightly with aluminum foil.
5. Bake the ribs for 23 hours, or until the meat is tender and almost falling off the bone.
6. While the ribs are cooking, prepare the sauce. In a medium saucepan, combine the beef

bone broth, tomato sauce, apple cider vinegar, honey, Worcestershire sauce, Dijon mustard, liquid smoke, and cayenne pepper.

7. Bring the sauce to a simmer over medium heat, stirring occasionally.
8. Reduce the heat to low and let the sauce simmer for about 1520 minutes, or until it thickens slightly.
9. Once the ribs are done cooking, remove them from the oven and carefully remove the aluminum foil.
10. Brush the ribs with the sauce, making sure to coat them evenly.
11. Preheat your grill to high heat. Place the ribs on the grill and cook for 57 minutes on each side, or until they are charred and crispy.
12. Serve the ribs hot, with any remaining sauce on the side. Enjoy!

Vanilla Panna Cotta

Ingredients:

- 1 cup unsweetened almond milk
- 1/4 cup powdered erythritol (or any other lowcarb sweetener)
- 1 tablespoon gelatin powder
- 1 cup heavy cream
- 1 teaspoon vanilla extract

Directions:

1. In a saucepan, heat the heavy cream and almond milk over medium heat until it's hot but not boiling.
2. Stir in the powdered erythritol until it's dissolved.
3. Sprinkle the gelatin powder over the liquid mixture and whisk it in quickly to avoid lumps.

4. Continue stirring until the gelatin is fully dissolved and the mixture is smooth.
5. Remove the saucepan from heat and stir in the vanilla extract.
6. Pour the Vanilla Panna Cotta mixture into individual serving cups or ramekins.
7. Refrigerate the panna cotta for at least 3 hours or until it's set.
8. Serve your Vanilla Panna Cotta chilled, and enjoy the creamy and lightly sweetened dessert!

Coconut Fat Bombs

Ingredients:

- 1/4 cup unsweetened shredded coconut
- 1/4 cup unsalted macadamia nuts, chopped
- 1/4 teaspoon vanilla extract
- 1/2 cup coconut oil, melted
- 1/4 teaspoon stevia extract (or any other lowcarb sweetener, to taste)

Directions:

1. In a bowl, mix the melted coconut oil, shredded coconut, chopped macadamia nuts, vanilla extract, and stevia extract until well combined.
2. Pour the Coconut Fat Bombs mixture into silicone molds or small paper cupcake liners.

3. Place the molds or liners on a baking sheet for stability.
4. Freeze the fat bombs for at least 1 hour or until they are solidified.
5. Pop the fat bombs out of the molds or liners and store them in an airtight container in the freezer.
6. Enjoy these Coconut Fat Bombs as a quick and satisfying snack, packed with healthy fats!

Baconchocolate Bark

Ingredients:

- 4 oz bacon, cooked until crispy and chopped
- 2 tablespoons unsweetened shredded coconut (optional)
- 4 oz dark chocolate (at least 70% cocoa), chopped

Directions:
1. Line a small baking sheet with parchment paper.
2. In a microwave safe bowl or a double boiler, melt the chopped dark chocolate until smooth.
3. Pour the melted chocolate onto the prepared baking sheet, spreading it out into an even layer.

4. Sprinkle the chopped bacon and shredded coconut (if using) over the melted chocolate.
5. Place the Bacon Chocolate Bark in the refrigerator for about 2030 minutes or until it's set.
6. Break the bark into pieces and store it in an airtight container in the refrigerator.
7. Enjoy the sweet and savory delight of this Bacon Chocolate Bark!

Gnocchi With Meat Ragout

Ingredients:

- 1/2 cup of red wine
- 1/2 cup meat stock
- 2 tablespoons olive oil
- Salt and pepper to taste
- Grated cheese for garnish
- 500 g of gnocchi
- 400 g ground meat (mixed beef and pork)
- 1 onion, finely chopped
- 2 cloves of garlic, finely chopped
- 400 g tomato pulp
- 2 tablespoons of tomato paste

- Chopped fresh parsley for garnish (optional)

Directions:

1. Start by preparing the meat sauce. In a skillet, heat the olive oil over medium heat and add the onion and garlic. Sauté until they become translucent.
2. Add the ground meat to the skillet and cook until well browned and free of liquid.
3. Add the tomato pulp, tomato paste, and red wine.
4. Stir well and cook over medium low heat for about 15 to 20 minutes, until the ragout has thickened.
5. Add the meat stock to the meat sauce and let it cook for another 5 minutes. Adjust salt and pepper to taste.
6. Meanwhile, bring a pot of salted water to a boil. Cook the gnocchi according to the Directions: on the package, until al dente.

Drain the gnocchi and add them to the meat sauce.

7. Stir gently to allow them to take on flavor with the meat sauce. Serve the gnocchi with meat sauce hot, garnishing with grated cheese and fresh chopped parsley if desired.

Lentil Soup With Sausage

Ingredients:

- 2 carrots, diced
- 2 celery stalks, diced
- 2 garlic cloves, finely chopped
- 1 bay leaf
- 1 liter of vegetable broth or meat stock
- 50 g dried lentils
- 2 sausages, skinned and crumbled
- 1 onion, finely chopped
- 2 tablespoons olive oil
- Salt and pepper to taste
- Chopped fresh parsley for garnish

Directions:

1. Start by rinsing the lentils under running water and draining them.
2. In a large pot, heat the olive oil over medium heat and add the onion, carrots, celery, and garlic. Sauté until the vegetables begin to soften.
3. Add the crumbled sausage to the pot and cook until well browned.
4. Add the lentils, bay leaf, and vegetable stock or meat broth.
5. Bring to a boil, then reduce the heat to medium low, cover the pot, and let it cook for about 30 to 40 minutes until the lentils are soft and tender.
6. Adjust salt and pepper to taste. Remove the bay leaf from the soup and serve hot, garnishing with fresh chopped parsley.

Risotto Alla Milanese With Ossobuco

Ingredients:

- 2 cloves of garlic, finely chopped
- 1/2 cup dry white wine
- 1.5 l of meat broth
- Saffron pistils (one sachet), 50 g of butter
- 50 g of grated parmesan cheese
- 320 g of carnaroli or arborio rice
- 4 veal ossobuco
- 1 onion, finely chopped
- Salt and pepper to taste.

Directions:

1. Start by preparing the ossobuco. In a large pot, heat some olive oil and add the onion and garlic. Saute until translucent.
2. Add the ossobuco to the pot and brown them on both sides until they are golden brown.
3. Add the white wine and let it evaporate for a few minutes. Add the beef broth to the pot, cover it with a lid, and cook over low heat for about 1 hour and 15 minutes, until the meat is tender and detaches easily from the bones.
4. Meanwhile, prepare the risotto. In a separate pot, melt the butter over medium heat.
5. Add the rice and toast it for a few minutes, stirring constantly. Add a ladleful of hot broth to the rice and stir until absorbed.
6. Continue adding the stock, a little at a time, stirring constantly, until the rice is al dente and creamy.

7. This should take around 1520 minutes. Add the saffron to the risotto and mix well to distribute it evenly.
8. Remove the ossobuco from the pot, remove the bone, and cut the meat into slices or stracciatella.
9. Add the ossobuco meat to the risotto and mix gently. Add the grated cheese to the risotto and stir until it melts completely.
10. Season with salt and pepper to taste. Serve the risotto alla Milanese with ossobuco hot, garnishing with a sprinkling of grated cheese.

Carnivore Fried Chicken Strips

Ingredients:

- 1.5 lbs chicken thighs
- 6 oz pork cracklings (or pork rinds, but pork cracklings work better)
- 2 eggs
- Sea salt (to taste)

Directions:
1. Make the breading.
2. Take the pork cracklings and blend them until they reach the consistency of an oily powder.
3. Note: Pork rinds will work too, however, I could not achieve as thick of a breading layer with pork rinds.
4. Place the pork crackling powder in a mediumsized bowl. Prepare the chicken

strips. Cut the chicken thighs into strips. I cut mine into strips that were about 4 inches long and 1/21 inch wide, but you can cut yours into whatever size you prefer. Make the fried chicken.

5. Beat two eggs in a small bowl. Dip each chicken strip into the egg mixture. Once fully coated, immerse it into the pork crackling powder and roll it around until it's fully coated with a thick layer.
6. The powder will be oily and should stick together. Make sure the breading layer is thick. Place the coated chicken strips onto a parchment paperlined baking sheet.
7. Salt them liberally. Bake for 20 minutes at 400 degrees, flip, then bake for another 2025 minutes.
8. The coating should be hard to the touch and crunchy when the chicken strips are finished.

9. I made these in my air fryer and the 20 min20 min at 400 degrees worked well.
10. Serve and enjoy! Make some OnionFree Guacamole, Honey Mustard, or Duck Fat Ranch Dressing for dipping. If you plan on saving them for later, store them in an airtight container in the fridge for 23 days.

Ultra Simple Carnivore Diet Bone Broth Recipe

Ingredients:

- 6 pounds beef bones

- ¼ cup raw apple cider vinegar optional

Directions:

1. Arrange the bones in a single layer in a large roasting tray and place them in the oven at 450°F (232°C) for about 20 minutes, until golden brown. NOTE: This step is optional and followed to affect the end flavor of the broth.
2. Place all the bones in a large stockpot. Fill with enough water to fully cover the material.
3. Pour in optional vinegar.
4. Bring the water to a boil, then reduce down to a simmer. Adjust the flame and pot lid to maintain a low simmer.
5. Cook for at least 18 hours, and up to 72 hours. I tend to pull my batch after about 24 hours.

Check periodically to ensure the water remains over the bones. Add extra water as needed.

6. Let the broth cool slightly. If a layer of scum or film appears over the top, skim it off with a slotted spoon. Strain the broth through a finemesh strainer or cheesecloth. Store in glass jars in the fridge for up to 5 days or in the freezer for longer.

www.ingramcontent.com/pod-product-compliance
Lightning Source LLC
LaVergne TN
LVHW010216070526
838199LV00062B/4609